CROWDED MOMENT

Morgan Brings The Civil War To Springfield

Colonel Arthur L. Kelly

The Clark Group

Lexington, Kentucky

Clark Publishing, Inc
dba The Clark Group
250 East Short Street
Lexington, KY 40507
800 944 3995 info@theclarkgroupinfo.com

Visit our Web site at www.TheClarkGroupInfo.com

First Edition: September 2010

Printed in the United States of America.
10 9 8 7 6 5 4 3 2 1

ISBN: 978-0-9827453-1-1

Book & cover design by Kelly Elliott
Special thanks to the University of Kentucky Archives and The Springfield Sun.

Dedication

To the descendants of the men who took part in the Morgan Christmas Raid into Kentucky. Both the Union and Confederate soldiers and especially those offsprings currently living in Washington and Marion Counties. And to my children, grandchildren, step-children, step-grandchildren, and great grandchildren, but most of all for my wife, Jane.

Prologue

On the dark night of December 30, 1862, 3900 Confederate cavalrymen overwhelmed the little Kentucky town of Springfield. In the cold and driving sleet, exhausted sons of the community—enemies now, yesterday's neighbors—faced off in deadly combat. In one tragic scene of mounted men locked in hand-to-hand fighting, one of Springfield's young sons watched another cherished son on the other side fall in his last second this side of heaven. The five hundred residents of Springfield were now experiencing the harsh realities of the Civil War.

Morgan Brings the Civil War to Springfield

On December 14, 1862, Confederate generals, distinguished guests, and kin folks, began arriving at the Ready mansion in Murfreesboro, Tennessee, to witness and celebrate John Hunt Morgan and Mattie Ready's wedding. In his Episcopal bishop's robe, Gen. Leonidas Polk performed the ceremony.

Outside the mansion, two military bands added to the festive affair. Later one band moved inside and played for the dancing couples. At the in-house reception the good southern food, drinks, and gala atmosphere dampened the tension and pressure felt by Gen. Braxton Bragg and the other military attendees who were concerned about Union battle plans for the immediate area. The brewing military situation would assure a fleeting honeymoon for the newly promoted brigadier general and General Morgan's beautiful twenty-one-year-old bride, Mattie.

John Hunt Morgan and Mattie, shortly after their wedding.
Courtesy of University of Kentucky Archives.

Just eight days after the wedding, Mattie Morgan stood beside her thirty-seven-year-old husband on the reviewing stand in Alexander, Tennessee, and watched the long line of mounted cavalryman in the general's regiments pass in company formations. The prancing horses and regimental colors flapping in the breeze made a magnificent scene. When all eyes of the passing riders focused on the young couple, it roused the Morgans' pride. Still, they felt the sadness of their imminent separation—Morgan had his orders to make another deep penetration into Kentucky.

Prior to this moment and after the big battle at Perryville, Kentucky, on October 8, 1862, the Union army had followed Bragg's army out of Kentucky and into Middle Tennessee. Morgan with a smaller cavalry force had supported Bragg's failed invasion of Kentucky. While there, Morgan had added recruits to his command and had made additional contacts with Southern sympathizers.

From Washington D.C., Pres. Abraham Lincoln had pressed his new commander in Tennessee, Gen. William Rosecrans, for action. But Rosecrans had informed the president by telegraph that some of his men were barefooted and that he needed delivery of clothes, weapons, and other critical items to his base in Nashville before he could go on the offence.

The 180-mile-long L&N railroad line between Nashville and Louisville was a main artery of supply for Rosecrans' plans. Consequently, he had allocated materials for forts at vulnerable places along the route and military forces to man the garrisons.

Morgan had cut the L&N supply artery in August 1862 by setting off massive explosions in the twin tunnels near Gallatin, Tennessee. This action, the raid into the bluegrass area of Kentucky in July of 1862, and other guerrilla-type operations, had already made the dashing young general a celebrity in the South.

Morgan had closed the tunnels for ninety-eight days. But now supplies were rolling into Nashville. Unaware of the situation, and thinking the railroad would soon be open, Bragg had ordered Morgan to enter Kentucky and destroy the L&N bridges, trestles, and telegraph lines along the route.

On December 22, 1862, one day after Morgan and Mattie reviewed the troops at Alexander, Morgan and his command, consisting of about 3900 cavalryman organized into two brigades, left the area for Kentucky. That night, the 1st Brigade, commanded by Morgan's brother-in-law, Col. Basil Duke, camped on the north bank of the Cumberland River at Sand Shoals, Tennessee.

Ninety percent of Morgan's men were from Kentucky and when they crossed the Kentucky boundary on Christmas Eve, James McCreary recorded, "Tonight we are camped on the sacred soil of old Kentucky and it fills my heart with joy." Other

Cpt. Patrick Simms. COURTESY OF CATHERINE TAYLOR CLEMENTS.

happy Kentuckians were forty Confederate cavalrymen from Springfield under the command of Cpt. Patrick Simms of Company K, 8th Cavalry Regiment. At this moment they did not know what lay ahead for them in their home town nor did they even know that they would be going to Springfield, Kentucky.

Already, Morgan was missing his beautiful bride, he wrote,

> *My Darling*
> *We reached this point [in Kentucky] last night after a long march & find everything ahead looks favorable. Shall reach Glasgow tonight & tomorrow hope to cross Green River. Shall then commence work upon the railroad & hope to get through with it by Sunday & then My Precious One I shall try to get back to you as fast as possible & then my pretty one nothing shall induce me to leave you again this winter . . . Farewell my Pretty Wife, my command is leaving & I must be off.*

On Christmas day, Morgan's long column snaked its way through Glasgow with his seven artillery pieces in tow. The artillery was the only thing on wheels. John Weathered's diary

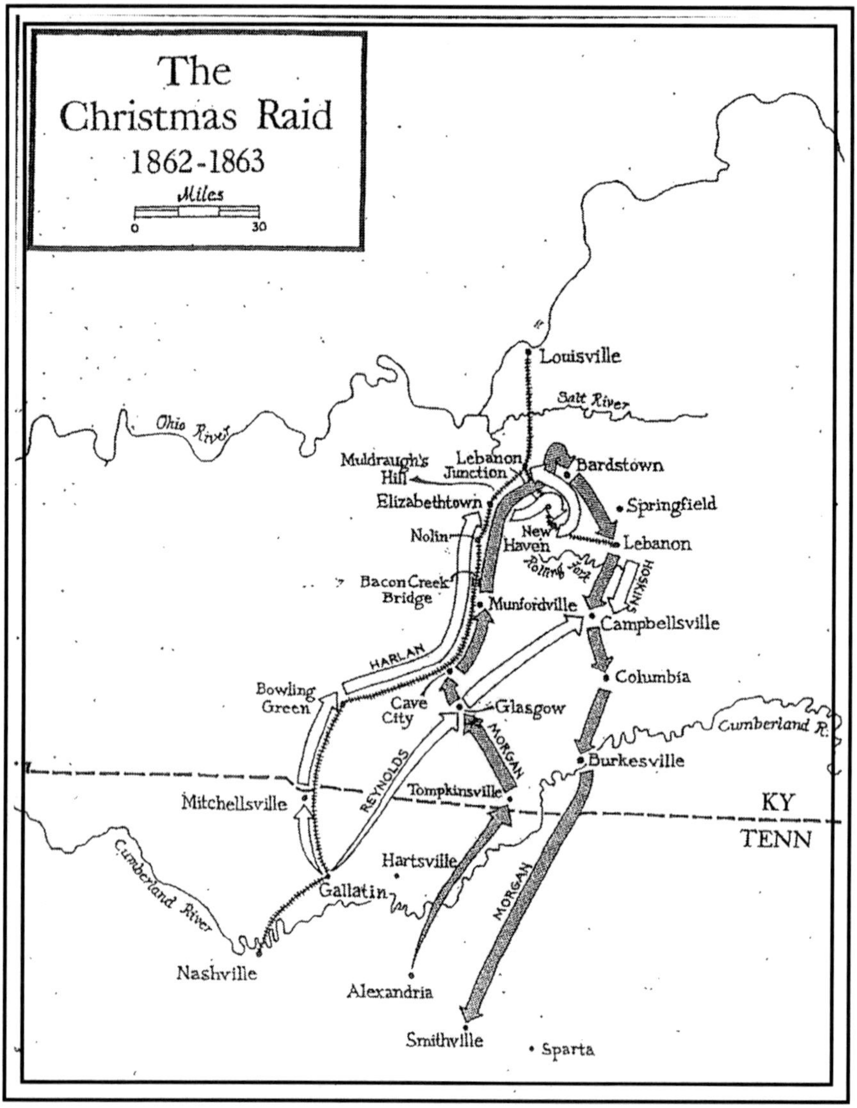

Courtesy University Press of Kentucky

John Marshall Harlan.
Justice of the United States Supreme Court 1877-1911.
MATTHEW BRADY, COLLECTION OF THE SUPREME COURT OF THE UNITED STATES.

recorded, "We marched early next morning (Christmas day) through Glasgow, the weather cold and stormy."

On December 26, while Morgan was busy overcoming stiff resistance at the Bacon Creek Railroad bridge north of Munfordville, Kentucky, Union forces began making their moves in Tennessee and Kentucky to save the L&N and to trap Morgan.

On that same day Col. John Marshal Harlan with his Union brigade, stuffed into railroad cars, forming three trains, steamed out of Gallatin, Tennessee. "He was to turn Morgan away from the L&N line and drive him back upon the forces converging in southern Kentucky to close off the Rebel retreat." (Ramage 1986 , 141).

On the trains and in hot pursuit of Morgan with Harlan's brigade, the 4th and 10th Infantry Regiments, each containing men from Springfield and Washington County. Thus men on opposite sides from the same county were in the chase. Harlan had organized and commanded the 10th prior to this operation and he played an active roll in recruiting Washington County

Col. Basil Duke. Courtesy of University of Kentucky Archives.

men for the unit. Mutual friends were also on opposite sides. Both Duke and his friend John Harlan graduated from Centre College. (Brewer 1997, 147).

On December 26, after Morgan's raiders captured and burned the L&N bridges at Bacon Creek and Nolin, they headed for Elizabethtown—burning crossties, heating and twisting rails, and destroying telegraph lines on the way. (Ramage 1986, 139).

While Morgan's wet and exhausted men moved toward their camp site just south of Elizabethtown, Harlan waited anxiously at Bowling Green for his third train. It was sidelined south of the tunnels awaiting an engine replacement.

On the morning of December 27th with his brigade intact, Harlan departed Bowling Green for Munfordville. Ten miles out, a train engine failed, creating another exasperating delay for Harlan who was anxious to save the two huge Muldraugh trestles northeast of Elizabethtown.

Meanwhile on that same morning, when Lt. Col. H. S. Smith, commanding the 652 Union soldiers at Elizabethtown, refused to surrender, Morgan deployed his troops south of the town, with Breckinridge's brigade on the left side of the road and Duke's on the right.

Duke describes the action: "I dismounted Cluke's regiment [8th-with Springfield men], and moved it upon the town, with its left flank keeping close to the road. I threw several companies, mounted, to the extreme right of my line, and the rear of the town. Breckinridge deployed his own regiment, under Lieutenant Colonel Stoner, immediately on the left of the road, stretching mounted companies to his left, and around the town" (Duke 1960, 333).

Duke continues:

> *The bulk of both brigades were in reserve. The parrot gun was placed in the pike; it was opened as soon as the last message from Colonel Smith was received; and, as suddenly as if its flash had ignited them, Palmer's four guns roared out from the hill [above the cemetery] on the left of the road, about 600 yards from the town where General Morgan himself was superintending their fire. Cluke moved warily, as two or three stockades were just in his front, which were thought to be occupied. When he entered the town he had little fighting to do, and that on the extreme right. Stoner dashed in on the left with the Ninth Kentucky, at a swift run. He burst into the houses occupied by the enemy at the edge of town, and with slight loss, compelled the inmates to surrender. The*

> *enemy had no artillery, and ours was battering the bricks about their heads in fine style. . . . Colonel Smith was not ready to surrender, but his men did not wait on him and poured out of the houses and threw down their arms.* (Duke 1960, 334).

After the battle, Morgan's men moved about the town destroying the railroad, burning the depot, rounding up horses worth taking, eating abandoned meals, entering open stores, and breaking in some that were not open for business. That afternoon before the 652 prisoners were paroled and marched off to Louisville, some of them had their boots and overcoats confiscated by their captors. Still many in the town were friendly to the rebels, providing them with meals and some with a bed to sleep in that night.

Not until 10:00 p.m. did Harlan reach Munfordville on the 27th. Here he learned that Morgan was north of the Green River and that the railroad bridges at Bacon Creek and Nolin had been destroyed. While Morgan's men slept, just thirty miles away at Elizabethtown, Harlan detrained his men. He reported later on, "wearied and fatigued by loss of sleep and the crowded condition of the cars . . ., [his men] lay upon the damp ground without tents to shelter them, to rest the best they could." Wishing desperately to catch Morgan before he destroyed the two high trestles at Muldraugh Hill, five miles northeast of Elizabethtown, Harlan roused his men and set out at 3:00 a.m. on foot.

Later on that morning on the 28th, Morgan left Elizabethtown, moving along the railroad toward the high trestles, his main objective. Thinking he was out of reach of Harlan, his command leisurely destroyed the railroad line along the way. The trestles, only a short distance apart, were about 500 feet long and around 80 feet high and hard to reach. Arriving at their objective around noon, Morgan assigned Duke to the upper trestle at Broad Run and Breckinridge to the lower trestle at Sulphur Fork. (Brewer 1997, 160).

After Lt. Col. Courtland Matson refused to surrender the two forts guarding the trestles, both Duke and Breckinridge opened fire with their artillery around 2:00 p.m. To escape the artillery pounding, some of the Indiana Union soldiers ran out of the fort into the woods. Pvt. John Wyeth, one of Morgan's scouts in Captain Quirk's Company, went looking for them and captured his first prisoner. He later wrote, "He seemed no older than myself, a good-looking lad with 'peachdown cheeks' which had tears trickling over them. His crying quickly aroused my sympathy, and I tried to reassure him by saying: 'Don't be afraid. Nobody shall harm you. You will be paroled now and can go home.' At this he sobbed out: 'I've got a good mother at home; and if I ever get back, I'll never leave her again.' By this time my own feelings were getting the best of me; and when he mentioned his mother, the thought of my own . . . never long out of my mind, overwhelmed me, and I began to cry too." (Wyeth 1911, 161).

Two hours into the fight, Matson surrendered his 560 men of the 71st Indiana Union Volunteers, and the raiders went to work gathering wood and kindling to burn the mighty trestles. The alternating snow and drizzle made the task a challenge, but when they finally got the massive and numerous wood poles and beams blazing, it made an awe-inspiring sight. When both structures came crashing down, Morgan had accomplished his main objective without suffering many casualties.

Meanwhile, Harlan's long column of 2900 men were moving as fast as they could on foot somewhere between Munfordville and Elizabethtown. That Sunday night on the 28th, Morgan's high-spirited command camped on the southern bank of the Rolling Fork near where the Elizabethtown-Bardstown Road crosses the river. While Morgan's men slept, Harlan's weary men pressed on, arriving at Elizabethtown early on Monday morning, December 29, 1862—where he received the bad news about the destruction of the trestles.

Upon learning that Morgan was camped on the river ten miles from Elizabethtown, Harlan continued the desperate pursuit hoping to save the bridges over the Rolling Fork. Harlan reported, "I marched immediately in that direction, ordering the cavalry to go far in advance. When I had gone about five

Morgan's raiders. Harper's New Monthly Magazine (August 1865).

miles . . . information reached me that the rebels were . . . at the place supposed . . . A section of Southwick's battery was ordered to join the cavalry, and, in conjunction with it, to detain the rebels at the crossing until the infantry arrived."

Under Morgan's command on that Monday morning, some 3900 mounted cavalry fanned out in all directions. Most of the main body plunged into the swift-swollen Rolling Fork River at the "Hamilton" ford south of the camp site and headed toward Boston on the Bardstown Road. Cluke's column with most of his 8th Regiment, a section of Palmer's Artillery, and Tom Quirk's Scouts moved on the south side of the river to the northwest from the camp site, with orders to destroy the railroad bridge about five miles down the river and near Lebanon Junction. After crossing the river to the north side, a portion of Stoner's 9th Kentucky Regiment along with an artillery section, rode southeast to attack the Union garrison at New Haven.

Unaware of Harlan's close proximity, Morgan, his two brigade commanders, and three of his regimental commanders were conducting a court-martial in the Hamilton house south of the road and camp site. Duke wrote, "we were leaving a brick house, on the southern side of the river and about six hundred yards from its bank, . . . the bursting of a shell . . . caught our ear. . . . This was about eleven a.m. We knew that a force of infantry and cavalry was cautiously following us, but did not know that it was so near. It was at once decided to throw into line the men who had not yet crossed, and hold the fords if possible, until Cluke's regiment could be brought back." (Duke 1960, 336).

Upon hearing his advanced element's artillery firing, Harlan ordered the infantry to move at the double-quick, and he galloped ahead of them to the front. In his report to General Boyle he wrote, "... from a high hill I saw quite distinctly a very large body of [enemy] cavalry formed in line of battle near the river. Their officers were riding along their line, apparently preparing to give us battle."

Duke was deploying his troops with their backs to the river in a rectangular meadow framed in woods on three sides. It had a natural depression across it that gave his troops protection and concealment, allowing him to move and expose his men in a way that exaggerated their numbers. To hold the crossing Duke placed the two remaining companies of Cluke's 8th Kentucky on the left, what was left of Stoner's 9th Kentucky on the right, and two companies of Gano's 3rd Kentucky in the center. Horseholders tried to shelter their horses in the woods on the left of the line.

Neither Harlan nor Duke knew the strength of their opposition. Duke thought Harlan had nearly 7,000 infantry and cavalry advancing toward him and feared that his defenders of the crossing site might be, "swept into the turbid river at our backs. . . . We were not idle during this advance, but the skirmishers were busy in the edges of the woods on our flanks and the men in the meadow were showing themselves with the most careful regard to an exaggerated idea being formed of their numbers." (Duke 1960, 337).

Harlan reported, "Knowing that Morgan had a larger force than I had I proceeded cautiously. . . . My men were formed in two lines; skirmishers were thrown out from both infantry and cavalry, covering our whole front."

Duke wrote, "When the enemy reached the edge of the woods which fringed the southern extremity of the meadow, and had pressed our skirmishers out of it and away from the brick-house and its out-buildings, the artillery was brought up and four or five guns were opened upon us [from Harlan's left]. (Duke 1960, 337).

Harlan's report continues, ". . . and [his brigade]was ordered to advance and engage the enemy, the whole line following in close supporting distance. The firing commenced, on the part of the rebels, on our left; it was promptly and vigorously responded to by my skirmishers and artillery."

While Harlan's artillery on Duke's right roared and flashed, Palmer's artillery galloped onto the meadow—coming from the Lebanon Junction Railroad Bridge. To distract Harlan, Duke ordered them to gallop across the front to the upper ford. Not wanting to get decisively engaged Duke ordered Palmer's six pounder cannons to make a rapid crossing and they plunged into the muddy-swift river. In the midst of these battle noises and confusion, Cluke's 8th Regiment detachment from the Lebanon Junction Bridge galloped on to the scene shouting at the top of their voices and they were quickly thrown into the line.

> *We [Duke] now wanted to cross with the entire force that was on the southern side, but this was likely to prove a hazardous undertaking with an enemy so greatly out-numbering us lying just in our front. . . . The enemy's guns-the best served of any, I think, that I ever saw in action-were playing havoc with the horses . . . and actually bursting shells in the lower ford with such frequency as to render the crossing at it by a column out of the question.* (Duke 1960, 338).

The odds were stacked against Duke with 800 men facing 2900 and he knew it. He wrote, "But when the enemy moved upon us again his infantry deployed in a long line, strongly supported, with a skirmish line in front, all coming on with bayonets glistening, the guns redoubling their fire, and cavalry column on the right flank [of Duke's line] apparently ready to pounce on us too, and then the river surging at our backs, my blood, I confess, ran cold." (Duke 1960, 338).

Duke had visions of his "gallant rear guard" being driven into the river or being bayoneted to death on its bank. With both his own life and the lives of his men in extreme danger, it was enough to make his blood run cold. But when the final moment seemed at hand, Harlan wavered.

With the pause of Harlan's line, Duke ordered a diversionary attack in the center, while Cpt. Virgil H. Pendleton with three companies of the 8th Kentucky Regiment attacked Harlan's two artillery cannons on the high ground on Duke's left. Duke wanted to silence the enemy artillery on his left and under the cover of these actions, he planned to gather his forces at the two fords for a rapid river crossing.

Just as Duke issued orders to execute his withdrawal plan, an artillery shell roared in and exploded with an ear-shattering blast. Two bleeding horses dropped in their tracts never to rise again and Duke tumbled to the ground with a serious head wound. Colonel Breckinridge immediately assumed command.

Some of the scouts scooped Duke's limp body off the ground and placed it astride the pommel of the saddle in front of Captain Quirk. With his arms wrapped around his beloved Colonel, Quirk guided his powerful bay horse into the cold, swift, and swollen river. Part way across another artillery round crashed down into the river. The loud explosion splashed water high and wide, splattering cold water over the scouts crossing the muddy water with their leader.

Wyeth wrote, "Another shell burst in the water as we were floundering across and splattered us. General Duke being unconscious, was the only man who wasn't scared." (Wyeth 1911, 187). At first, word mistakenly spread through Morgan's com-

Col. William Hays, Springfield, Kentucky, commander of the 10th Kentucky Volunteer Infantry (Union) during the Civil War. About 400 men from Washington County served under him.

mand that General Duke had been killed. The report saddened and concerned the raiders.

While Breckinridge directed the execution of the withdrawal plan, Harlan made his move. After the action, Harlan in his report to General Boyle wrote, "After a while the rebels were driven away, and they then made some demonstrations to occupy an eminence upon my right. . . . a section of the battery was ordered to occupy the eminence, and the 10th Kentucky, Lieutenant Colonel [William] Hays, ordered to support it."

Colonel Hays, a Springfield, Kentucky, native, had Springfield men in four of his companies deployed against the Confederate 8th Regiment, which also included Springfield men. In addition, there were Springfield men in the 4th Kentucky Infantry Regiment of Harlan's brigade facing the rebels rear guard.

Meanwhile across the river, a carriage was impressed and a soft bedding was made for the raider's unconscious brigade commander, to comfort him as they moved him toward Bardstown.

The limited attack on Harlan's artillery on the high ground, drove the cannoneers from the guns and silenced them for about thirty minutes. While leading the charge, Captain Pendleton of the Confederate's 8th Regiment was badly wounded by a shell fragment.

On the ground around the silent guns lay Lt. Henry W. Pollis, an artilleryman, and Pvt. Louis W. Finney, an infantryman—both mortally wounded. Nearby lay Thomas Burton, Company F, Fourth Kentucky Volunteers, killed in action. Only Harlan's men lay on the ground.

With the guns on the high ground temporarily out of action and having found a new fording site behind Cluke's 8th Regiment at the last minute, Breckinridge hastily gathered his rear guard and sent them dashing into the swollen river and out of the trap, leaving behind ten dead horses. All of his wounded men rode out with the rear guard.

Duke wrote, "Aided by this diversion [the attack on the high ground] and the one made on the front, everything was suddenly thrown into columns and [we] dashed across the river, leaving the army on the other side cheated of its prey which it ought too have secured." (Duke 1960, 339).

Unaware that he was only facing Morgan's rear guard, Harlan failed to press his advantage aggressively. He reported,

". . . but the rebels, after an obstinate resistance, broke and fled precipitately in every direction. Some struck out into the woods; some went up the river as far as New Haven; some swam the river with their horses."

After the rebels managed to cross the river, Harlan chose not to pursue the raiders to give some rest to his men suffering from extreme exhaustion and sleep deprivation. At 11:30 p. m. (Monday, December 29th) his scout returned with news that the Rolling Fork Bridge was still standing. He roused his weary and sleepy men and started for the bridge about five miles down the river. Before daylight, they arrived at the bridge and encamped on the south side of it. He reported his situation to Gen. Jeremiah Boyle, who ordered him to protect the bridge and be prepared to defend the long bridge over the Salt River at Shepherdsville.

Safely across the river, the rear guard fell in behind Morgan's long column now on the road moving toward Bardstown. Wyeth wrote, "Our company was now ordered to ride through the command and take the lead, which we did, reaching Bardstown at dusk, where we found shelter in a livery stable and a sound sleep on a corn-pile." (Wyeth 1911, 187).

As the long river of horses with their mounts flowed into Bardstown, cavalrymen began swarming in and around the town. A few were fed by family or friends of their cause. Some shopped for food and gifts for love ones. Duke's carriage arrived and was guided to Doctor Cox's home, where the unconscious leader was carried upstairs and streched out on a bed. When J.W. Cunningham, a well-known circuit preacher, bent over to observe the wound behind Duke's ear, Duke opened his eyes and said, "That was a pretty close call." (Brown 1975, 13).

Outside on the street, discipline broke down. Doors of the county jail were thrown open. Several Southern sympathizers accused of stealing horses burst out of jail and disappeared in the crowd. Some raiders burglarized the post office—took money and scattered letters in the streets. Rather than take any more worthless Confederate currency, one store owner quickly closed his store, locked the door, and disappeared. Early in the morning a surging crowd of angry raiders broke into the closed store and emptied the shelves. Wyeth wrote, "Within a short half-hour nothing but the shelves and counters were left, for in the riot of an uncontrolled desire to plunder these men took piles of stuff they could not carry away or use." (Wyeth 1911, 188).

On Tuesday, December 30, 1862, dawn broke clear and cold. In the lead and in high spirits, Quirk's scouts moved out for Springfield. While on the march, Lt. Frank Brady, entertained his comrades by singing the popular song, "The Years Creep Slowly By, Lorena."

In Lebanon, Col. W.A. Hoskins, commanding the expedition force assembling there, got busy gathering information and making plans to engage Morgan. He did not know the size of Morgan's force. He had estimates anywhere from 3,000 to 11,000.

On Monday the 29th, while the battle had been raging at the Rolling Fork River, Hoskins had sent a small cavalry party under Lieutenant Samuel Porter with orders to "proceed in the direction of New Haven and Bardstown until he could learn something definite of Morgan's force and movement." He also sent a citizen-scout in the direction of Springfield and Bardstown with similar instructions. At Frederickburg [Fredericktown] on Tuesday morning, the citizen-scout had breakfast with fifteen of Morgan's raiders and then hurried back and reported his discovery.

As the morning wore on, more and more of Morgan's regiments and companies flowed out of Bardstown into the stream of cavalrymen moving toward Springfield. Soon the sun disappeared behind the gathering clouds. By noon, a chilly drizzle sprinkled the riders and their horses as they moved along at a slow gait. About 3 o'clock, advanced elements rode into Springfield.

About the same time that day, Lieutenant Porter arrived in Lebanon and confirmed the civilian-scout's report and reported that the cannonading they had heard the day before had been at Rolling Fork.

With that information Hoskins ordered out two

reconnaissances in force. Lt. Col. John Boyle led a strong detachment from his 9th Kentucky Cavalry toward Raywick, while Col. Dennis Halisy, from Washington County, led cavalrymen from his 6th Kentucky Regiment toward Springfield. To make his final battle plans, Hoskins needed to know whether Morgan would approach Lebanon from Springfield, Raywick, or from both directions.

As the gray, dreary day wore on and the temperature continued to drop, Morgan's long column grew shorter and shorter as his wet, cold, and weary cavalrymen rode into town filling the streets of Springfield and spilling out onto the Lebanon Road. Soon Stoner's detachment joined them from New Haven, where the defenders of the railroad bridge had repulsed the raider's attack.

With night approaching on that Tuesday, the reconnaissance party of the 6th Regiment returned, and Halisy reported that Morgan had been found encamped on the Springfield-Lebanon road.

Initially, Hoskins wanted to go on the offensive and attack Morgan at Springfield. But unsure of Morgan's strength and knowing that Harlan had chosen not to pursue Morgan after the action at Rolling Fork, Hoskins decided to go on the defensive. He chose the high ground in the angle formed by the Cartwright Creek and the Springfield Road north of Lebanon. In his after-action report he said, "I had on the evening of December 30, selected a position for one section of the battery... This position commanded the Springfield Road for 1 ½ miles, and was strengthened by a precipitous bluff on the right flank. At this point I felt we must meet the enemy; for, if they were permitted to pass it, and gain possession of a copse of timber and the commanding position on the hill, they could shell us in town . . ." (Morgan's Second Kentucky Raid, Dec. 1862, 144).

Shortly after Halisy's report, Hoskins received information that Morgan planned to split his forces and send 2,000 raiders out of Springfield onto the Haysville Road [present Simmstown-Perryville-Springfield Road]. The validity of that information was critical for his plans to defend Lebanon. He wrote, "To ascertain the truth . . ., I ordered out detachments from the Sixth, and Ninth Kentucky Cavalry, under command of Major Fidler and Farris to reconnoiter in the direction of Barber's [Barbour's] Mill, with instruction that, if the enemy had not passed that point, to take the Springfield road and reconnoiter in their rear. (Morgan's Second Kentucky Raid, Dec 1862, 144).

Both the 9th and 6th had Springfield men in their ranks. According to a report to the Kentucky Adjutant General, dated September 29, 1863, and signed by eleven Washington County officials, Halisy's 6th Regiment had 200 men in its ranks from the county and the 9th had 40. In the report they declared that the numbers given were "the best we can arrive at."

By nightfall, the cold drizzle gradually turned first into freezing rain and then into beads of sleet adding to the misery of all the troops exposed to the elements, especially the large number of men out on the Lebanon Road. But a few managed to find temporary relief. John Castleman, one of the raiders, wrote, "Lieutenant George B. Eastin . . . had the privilege of being numbered among a lot of confederate soldiers who were enjoying a 'square meal' at the hospitable home of Mr. Cunningham. There were present several charming young women. . . . One of the most attractive young ladies made the proposition that she would marry any confederate soldier who killed Halisy. Eastin, with his accustomed courtesy, rose from his chair and accepted the challenge." (Castleman 1917, 109). While Halisy, an M.D., was admired by the local citizens on the Union side, he was detested by the county secessionists.

Outside of the Cunningham house on that cold, wet, and dark night, the little town of 500 citizens—mostly Union sympathizers—found itself full of and surrounded by about 3900 cold-exhausted-rebel cavalrymen, their horses, and captured wagons loaded with supplies and artillery. Early in the night as the tail of the column drifted in, Springfield came alive. Shouting, bitching, laughing, and with the horses coming and going filled the airwaves with different sounds.

Upon arriving one squad went to a stable, fed their horses, but left their saddles on. One of the raiders reported, " I went to a house across the street with others and got supper. The boys made a fire in the stable's yard. . . . The ground was wet so we laid some new plank near the fire and took a short nap."

In Springfield, Morgan began receiving grim intelligence. He received word that his enemy had withdrawn forces from Danville, Burkesville, Campbellsville, and Columbia and had concentrated a force of 8,000 at Lebanon. Intelligence also reached him that a column of about 10,000 strong was moving from Glasgow to Burkesville to intercept him before he could cross the Cumberland River and return to his safe base in Tennessee. And he knew Harlan was behind him.

Although Colonel Henderson and his two regiments from Danville were recalled before they got to Lebanon, Morgan was still in a dangerous situation. To add to his apprehension, the deteriorating weather was foreboding, the night was pitch dark, and the troops were exhausted. Still he made an agonizing decision to make a night march around Lebanon on poor and little-used roads between the town and Saint Mary's.

In his after-action report he wrote, "In this emergency, I determined to make a detour to the right of Lebanon, and by a night march, to conceal my movement from the enemy, . . . at Springfield, I sent out two companies on the Lebanon Road with instructions to drive in the enemy's pickets, and to hold the position." (Morgan's Second Kentucky Raid, Dec. 1862, 157).

Meanwhile in Springfield, rebel James B. McCreary found warmth, food and hospitality at the McElroys. He recorded in his war-time journal,

> *December 30. Reached Springfield late at night, tired and very hungry. Ordered supper at McElroys. There met Sanders, an old class mate. Had an excellent supper. While I was enjoying it, an order came for me to take three companies, move out on Lebanon Road, drive in enemy's pickets, and make a feint. Hurried through with supper. Moved my command through sleet and cold to the aforesaid road. Found the enemy [pickets] not over a mile from our camp. Drove them with almost continual fighting two miles. Then built many fires as a feint.*

But before Morgan could move 3900 mounted cavalrymen, their acquired wagon train and artillery over little-used, muddy roads that continued to get slicker from accumulating sleet, he had to find competent guides. Deadly and frustrating delay dragged on as he searched for them.

Out on the Haysville Road near Barber's [Barbour] Mill, having discovered that Morgan wasn't in the area, Major Fidler selected Cpt. Edward Penn, Lieutenant Murphy, and fifty men of the 6th Cavalry Regiment and proceeded toward Springfield.

In Springfield, while exhausted raiders in their camps in and around town try to catch a little restless sleep in the arena of the freezing, piercing wind and sleet, Morgan and his staff absorb themselves in planning for the night march and issuing orders for the execution of the difficult task. Couriers are moving about in the darkness between command headquarters with instructions and information.

In the center of Springfield, a rebel artillery battery, "planted in the streets" and sheeted with ice, remained silent while the exhausted and miserable cannoneers tried to snatch a little rest.

Out on the Haysville-Perryville Road, Major Fidler with his 6th Cavalry Regiment detachment, carefully approached Springfield, surprised and captured an inattentive rebel picket.

Under the cover of total darkness, and with the distraction of the near blizzard conditions, Fidler discreetly penetrated the rebel encampment and boldly led his men down East Main Street to the vicinity of the courthouse within fifty yards of the rebel artillery battery.

Hoskins reported, [they] "fired a volley in to the midst of the enemy, killing 2 of their number. . . ." Having revealed to the rebels that an enemy was in the middle of their encampment, Fidler hurriedly led his men out of the jaws of death and returned to Lebanon with his prisoner of war and valuable information for Hoskins. Hoskins said in his official report, "Major Fidler performed a feat of daring which is worthy of the highest praise . . . ."

Frank Taylor's 1992 painting - "Buell Departing for Perryville." In 1858, Hugh McElroy bought this house known as Elmwood from William Davison. On December 30, 1862, Morgan's raiders camped in the area out on the Springfield-Lebanon Road. While Major James McCreary was eating supper at the McElroy's—most likely here at Elmwood—he received orders to drive in the Lebanon defender's pickets and build fires to mask Morgan's intentions to make a night march around Lebanon.
COURTESY COL. AND MRS. ARTHUR L. KELLY

Maj. James McCreary, future two-time governor of Kentucky. COURTESY UNIVERSITY OF KENTUCKY ARCHIVES.

In Lebanon after Hoskins learned from Fidler and Farris that Morgan was not on the Springfield-Haysville Road, he sent by courier orders for Colonel Henderson to join him in Lebanon. After learning to his horror that Henderson had left the Bethel Church area with his two regiments for Danville, he knew the possibility of attacking Morgan in the morning at Springfield was definitely gone.

Out on the Lebanon-Springfield Road, after driving Hoskins' pickets back for two miles, Maj. James McCreary and his men got busy building many fires as ordered. Morgan wanted Hoskins to think his forces were staying encamped between Lebanon and Springfield while he made his night march around Lebanon. McCreary said, "It was bitter cold but it was certain death to stand before the firelight." The pickets on both sides grappled with each other for suitable terrain for their purposes. Both sides suffered a few casualties out on the picket lines.

Meanwhile, Morgan had rounded up his guides. He reported, "Considerable delay was occasioned from the difficulty in obtaining guides who were sufficiently well acquainted with the country to lead me over the route I desired to march, but at length, by 11 p.m. the whole column was fairly in motion. The night was dark and stormy and the road rough and intricate, . . ." (Morgan's Second Kentucky Raid, Dec. 1862, 153).

Among the guides was one of Springfield's respected citizens. The January 8, 1863, edition of the Louisville Daily Journal reported, "Morgan took a very worthy old citizen—a hotel keeper in Springfield named J. C. Rollins [Rawlins] with him. We feel sure that General Boyle will hold the Springfield rebels responsible for his safety. Let it be understood that two or three prominent ones will suffer if he is in danger."

By 9:00 p.m. lead elements moving toward Lebanon, leaning into swirling snow alternating with beads of sleet, turned their horses to the right a little ways out of Springfield, onto a little-traveled road leading to the Springfield-Elizabethtown Pike.

During that cold-dark night, while Springfield was being overwhelmed by 3900 raiders, their horses, and all the actions taking place in and around the town, some of its own rebel sons in Cpt. Patrick Simm's Company K were being captured. Included among the seven rebels of Company K who were taken prisoners, and who had previously enlisted in Company K in Springfield, were William McCormick, H.F. Lanham, Raphiel Shockency, and four Montgomerys—John, James, Robert, and Parker.

As the string of horses unwinds out of Springfield onto the dark byroad, maintaining the column's integrity and motion becomes a supreme task. If the column develops gaps and portions of the command gets hopelessly lost that creates long delays, it would create a dangerous situation for Morgan's command. He knows he has to beat the Union Forces to the Cumberland River crossing at Burkesville, Kentucky.

Out on the old Elizabethtown Pike a few miles from Springfield, the creeping column left the pike and headed south in the general direction of Saint Mary's. Teams of horses sloshing through mud and ice while pulling artillery pieces along often got stuck, further delaying the column.

As the night wore on, sleet pelted the weary raiders in the face unmercifully. Shouts rang out up and down the column, now stretching out for miles, "Keep moving—close up." Some sleep deprived and chilled rebels dismounted, grabbed onto a stirrup and slipped and stumbled beside their horses that were also slipping and sliding. Fatigue turned into extreme exhaustion. Cold-sleepy-spent men dropped out and built fires against orders.

John Wyeth wrote about that awful night.

> *What with the bitter, penetrating cold, the fatigue, the overwhelming desire to sleep, so difficult to overcome, and, under the conditions we were experiencing, so fatal if yielded to, the numerous halts to get the artillery out of bad*

places, the impenetrable darkness, and inevitable confusion . . ., we put in a night of such misery and anxiety and suffering that no man who experienced it could ever forget. (Wyeth 1911, 189).

It took insight and resolve to put the command on the road under the circumstances and great leadership to accomplish that most difficult task. Duke wrote, "The column floundered along blindly; the men worn out and half frozen, the horses stumbling at every step—nothing preserved organization and carried the column along but the will of the great Captain [Morgan] in the front and the unnerving sagacity which guided him." (Duke 1960, 341).

Later that night, out in the ever-lengthening column, as the temperature continued to drop, men's boots froze to their

stirrups. Exhausted men sheeted with ice shivered from the cold. Numbed hands dropped weapons never to be found in the darkness. Keeping one another awake required ceaseless effort.

At a stable in Springfield, about one o'clock in the morning, raider Curtis Burke got orders to mount up and fall in. The column, now strung out for miles, was emptying Springfield of its uninvited rebels and their horses.

Embers from abandoned fires, fueled by wooden fence rails, radiated little patches of heat in and around Springfield. When the raiders had found a good horse they had exchanged it for their worn-out horses. In the darkness out in the fields, broken-down rebel horses stood with their tails turned into the driving sleet. But grayclads didn't find twelve-year-old Will McChord's pony. Will wrote, "Morgan's men swiped every horse that could

William C. McChord, Washington County Attorney, wrote an eye witness account of local events during the Civil War.

be used in the cavalry service, yet, Flash was never found, although soldiers, in hunting for horses, on several occasions went around the plump thicket [where he hid his pony]." (W. C. McChord's Memoirs).

Meanwhile out on the road, exhausted raiders covered with a sheet of ice grew sleepier as they plodded along in the night. Wyeth wrote, "I remember passing a small cabin near the roadside and seeing the gleam of the fire from the hearth under the door, and I felt then as if I would give everything I had in this world . . . just for the privilege of lying down in front of that blaze and going to sleep . . . . Finally I became so numb that I could not hold my gun and somewhere in the darkness it dropped from my hands and was lost." (Wyeth 1911, 163).

In Lebanon—in the wee hours of the morning—Maj. L. A. Gratz of the 6th Cavalry returned from a late night patrol and reported that the enemy had advanced two miles in the direction of Lebanon. To determine whether Morgan was moving toward Lebanon to attack his position, Hoskins ordered Colonel Halisy to make another reconnaissance out on the Springfield Road. Halisy departed about 7:00 a.m. on December 31.

At last, day dawned. Raiders making their way around Lebanon were shocked at their own ghostlike appearance from the sheet of ice covering both riders and horses. Some were surprised to learn they had traveled in a circle. All night the column had moved at a snail's pace, often waiting while men labored to free their artillery stuck in the bad places along the ill-kept-dirt roads. Exhausted, sleepy men had caught cat naps as best they could.

John Weathered recorded, "I lost my horse Jimmie last night, I got off my horse and set down against a fence and went to sleep and when I woke up Jimmie was gone. I walked some and rode some behind the boys . . ."

Morgan reported, "The morning of December 31 found the command only 8 miles from Springfield and 2 1/2 miles from Lebanon." (Morgan's Second Kentucky Raid, Dec. 1862, 157).

Still the exhausted-sleepy raiders pressed on, heading for Campbellsville in a race to beat the Union forces to the Cumberland River crossing site at Burkesville. Soon traffic jams were broken and separated elements began rejoining their parent units and the pace picked up. A few miles South of Lebanon the head of the column entered the Lebanon-Campbellsville pike.

In Lebanon at 11:00 a.m., Halisy's messenger galloped into

town with word to Hoskins that Morgan's camp sites in and around Springfield were empty.

About noon, excited citizens hurried into Lebanon. Hoskins reported, "Citizens came rushing into town with the most extravagant reports regarding Morgan's force, and assuring us that he was advancing on the place, with his right column moving from the direction of Saint Mary's Church, on the Lebanon Branch Railroad." (Morgan's Second Kentucky Raid, Dec. 1862, 144).

Hoskins alerted his two brigade commanders and ordered out another reconnaissance to see if Morgan was coming. Lieutenant Colonel Boyle hurriedly left town with 300 troops of his 9th Kentucky Cavalry. Later on—without any word from Halisy since his eleven o'clock message—Hoskins, who admired Halisy's zeal and courage, felt considerable anxiety. But out on Morgan's trail, Halisy was aggressively chasing Morgan's rear guard and rounding up stragglers and sending the prisoners back to Lebanon. With the passage of time, Halisy's force grew smaller and smaller.

Galloping along behind the rebels rear guard, Halisy sighted a horseless stagecoach. Rebel troops placing old, wooden fence rails in the mail coach, looked up, saw the charging union cavalry and quickly dropped what they were doing and scurried off. Edmund Davison, a Springfield citizen, and part owner of the mail route and coach wrote of the event, "He [the rebel officer] then took the horses and ordered his men to burn the stage. Just as they had thrown a lot of old rails in the stage and was setting fire on it, a union officer, Major Halasey [Colonel Halisy], with a squad of soldiers came dashing upon them. They retreated . . . He [Halisy] was a very small man . . . and was very reckless and brave, often attacking the enemy many times greater than his force." (Davison 1901, 21).

At the head of his long rebel column, Morgan led his exhausted command across the Rolling Fork River and up the mighty Muldraugh Hill, a long escarpment that runs across much of central Kentucky. He reported, "By 1 o'clock that afternoon, however, the top of Muldraugh's Hill was reached , where I could see Lebanon with a glass [field glasses] distinctly, and the enemy's skirmishers deployed in the valley below."

On a noble steed that he had captured from the rebel Captain Carter along the way, and with a determination to carryout Hoskins' orders, to hang upon Morgan's rear and harass him to a stand, Halisy pressed on toward the Rolling Fork River with only John Edwards, his orderly, and Lt. Turner W. Bottoms close enough to help him.

Near New Market, as the sun was sinking fast, Halisy spotted three rebels ahead of them entering the main road through a gate. Reining in their horses, they exchanged fire with the rebels before the rebels galloped off down a straight lane opposite the gate. Daring death, Halisy and his men turned into the lane and the deadly chase was on.

Up ahead, rebel Cpt. Alexander Tribble, Lt. George Eastin, and a Morgan straggler fired their pistols over their shoulders in a running duel with their pursuers. In an area known as the lagoons just south of the river, west of the town, and near the Tile Factory Ford, the rebels leaning forward over thundering hoofs dropped down out of sight. Spotting an advantageous place Eastin turned a sharp corner and reined in his mount. Unable to make the sharp turn in time, Tribble splashed into the knee-deep, water-logged lagoon before he could stop his horse. The straggler continued on.

Out of sight of Halisy, Bottoms, and Edwards for a brief moment—two rebels waited.

Thundering ahead of the pursuers, Edwards spotted Eastin, tried desperately to rein in his horse, but couldn't, and ran squarely up to Tribble. Facing each other, both fired their pistols—both missed. Splashing hooves brought the clamoring combatants within reach of each other. With the Muzzle of his pistol against Edward's body, Tribble pulled the trigger. It snapped. Now to his consternation he stood at death's door. Desperately, the strong and quick Tribble—grunting and snorting—latched onto Edwards before he could fire and dragged him backward, off his restive horse. Locked in a death grip, both men tumbled off their mounts and splashed into the cold water.

Meanwhile galloping at full speed just behind Edwards, Halisy straining hard, managed to rein in his horse and stop just

Lt. George Eastin. COURTESY UNIVERSITY OF KENTUCKY ARCHIVES.

ten paces from his enemy. Eastin took aim—pulled the trigger—missed Halisy on his prancing horse—and hollered out "Surrender!" Halisy—aimed—fired—and missed. While the loud cracking noise echoed through the valley, Eastin moved a little closer and fired his pistol again. The speeding bullet knocked dust off Halisy's shoulder, but it didn't hurt him. The shouting, the furry, the loud shots are attracting the attention of the local civilians. Halisy returns fire and misses. Eastin spurred his reluctant horse forward within ten feet of Halisy and leveled his pistol on him. Halisy threw up his hands before Eastin could fire again and shouted, "I am your prisoner, sir. I am your prisoner!"

Moving closer to Halisy, Eastin's restless horse whirled around so that both horses faced in the same direction, side by side. Reaching out, Eastin demanded Halisy's pistol. Without warning, Halisy dropped his bridle reins and grabs Eastin by the collar with his left hand. And the mortal struggle resumes.

One or the other must die. Without taking careful aim, Halisy reaches up under his left arm and, with the muzzle of his pistol nearly touching Eastin's check, pulled the trigger but missed. Stunned by the ear-splitting blast and temporarily blinded by the flash, and with his face burning and blackened, Eastin instinctively grappled with his foe. Reaching out, he placed his pistol to Halisy's temple and fired. The fatal bullet ripped through the Federal's face, entering about an inch and a half above his upper lip and slightly to the right of his nose. The muzzle so close that the flash seared Halisy's eye-brows off.

Dazed from the struggle and with ears' ringing, Eastin subconsciously held on to Halisy's limp body while the horses moved side by side out of control into the pool of water—where the Tribble and Edward fight had by now ended. In the pool coming to his senses, Eastin released his dead adversary and reached for the bridle of Halisy's horse. The Yankee's lifeless body with its bloody, disfigured face slid down between the horses and splashed into the water. Somehow, his head got tangled up in the loose bridle rein of Eastin's horse, causing the animal to jump around as it plunged through the water, pulling the corpse along toward the other bank. On the bank the rein released the body, where it lay wet, still, and silent.

In the middle of Halisy's fight to the death, Tribble managed to get on top of Edwards and, after nearly drowning him, got him to surrender.

No sooner had Eastin collected his wits and taken in Tribble's situation, then all of a sudden Lieutenant Bottoms came charging around the corner. By now, Eastin's pistol was empty and he knew it. Nevertheless, Eastin aimed his pistol at his new foe and demanded that he surrender. Taking in the circumstances, Bottoms yielded and gave up. (*Southern Bivouac,* 1882, 121-125).

Nearby, rebel Oscar Walker, a Washington County native and member of Captain Simms' Company K, 8th Cavalry—having watched the thrashing about in the water, hearing the shouts, groans, and pistol shots—sat silently on his horse for a brief moment as he observed Halisy's wet, bloody corpse lying on the bank. Thus the civil war had brought two Kentucky cavalrymen on opposite sides from the same county together as a deadly tragedy played out. Judge Sam Boldrick of Springfield said, "Oscar Walker of Springfield was with Eastin and saw Halisy fall." (S. J. Boldrick, Letter to O. W. Baylor, 1939).

In a log house about a half-mile from the action, ten-year-old Mary Jane Bowman [later Mrs. William Buckman] had heard the shots and shouts echoing through the valley. She and her parents, Thomas and Nancy, rushed to the site of the calamity, where the road crosses the lagoon and observed Halisy's body lying on the bank of the lagoon. (*Lebanon Enterprise,* February 22, 1935).

After the fight ended, Eastin took Halisy's sword before

moving on with Tribble and their two prisoners. Riding along at a faster clip, they soon caught up with their command.

Back at the lagoon, Halisy's wet body with the gaping hole in his face was gently removed to a nearby house. On New Year's Day, his body was taken to the Campbell House in Lebanon, where it lay in state. Sympathetic ladies placed fresh flowers around his brow.

Col. Dennis J. Halisy was admired by the Union supporters. One obituary read, " He dared danger and beckoned death . . . . In him the country loses a noble defender, a valiant and glorious patriot, a scholar and a most worthy citizen. . . . He was . . . a native of Florida—true, courageous and brave—a pure citizen, a devoted catholic, . . . and a splendid scholar."

The *Louisville Daily Journal,* dated January 13, 1863, in a long obituary praising Colonel Halisy said, "We never knew a better physician . . . . As a scholar he was widely known. He spoke with fluency in nearly all of the modern European languages. . . . He abhorred treason in its every shape and shade—was quick to discern it, and as quick to punish it. And because of this, he was disliked by every rebel in the country."

But he was not disliked in the little village of Manton, Washington County, Kentucky where Doctor Halisy had practiced medicine. They mourned the loss of their beloved physician, who had served their medical needs. Early in the war he had recruited several of Manton's sons for Col. John Marshall Harlan's 10th Kentucky Volunteer Infantry.

There is another version of the incident. Most of the above account of the Halisy/Eastin's hand-to-hand fight is based on George Eastin's version of what happened. One reporter wrote,

> *Immediately after capturing them, Colonel Halisy was shot dead by a rebel officer, ... a citizen named Capeheart reached the ground directly after the colonel fell and asked the rebel officer [Eastin] why he killed him. The officer replied, 'The g-d son of a b-h shot at me twice after I captured him.' A mostinfamous lie, ... We do not doubt the infernal rogues (they robbed Halisy of his valuables and pulled off his hat and boots after killing him), killed him intentionally after capturing him."* (*Louisville Daily Journal,* January 6, 1863).

On January 1, 1863, Colonel Harlan in a dispatch to Gen. J. T. Boyle stated, "Colonel Halisy, Sixth Kentucky Cavalry, was murdered last night by Morgan's men; ... Was shot after he had surrendered, by a rebel officer." (Morgan's Second Kentucky Raid, Dec. 1862, 136).

In a news article in the *Louisville Daily Journal,* dated January 2, 1863 a reporter wrote, "I have just talked with Lieut. Bottom, who was with him [Halisy] when he was killed. He says that Col. H. [Halisy] was killed bravely fighting. Lieut. Eason [Eastin] of Mason County, shot him. They were so close to gather that Col. Halisy's eyelids and eyebrows were burnt off by the flash of the pistol. F."

Meanwhile back in Lebanon, Hoskins—unaware of the deadly hand-to-hand fight going on between Halisy and

Eastin—learned from his returning reconnaissance party that Morgan's main body had passed Saint Mary's Depot. He immediately started in pursuit with his two brigades, artillery and the two cavalry regiments with Springfield, Kentucky, men in their ranks (6th and 9th).

Upon arriving at a point near New Market, Hoskins received the sad news of Halisy's death. In his after action report he said, "Here we were informed by a citizen of the death of the gallant . . . and lamented Colonel Halisy, whom I could admire for his great zeal . . . By his death the service has lost one of its most . . . chivalrous officers, and the community one of its most useful and honorable citizens."

Late in the evening on Wednesday, December 31, Morgan's exhausted command arrived at Campbellsville. After his hungry men feasted on the Union army's commissary stores found there, they bedded down for the night.

Early on New Year's Day, Morgan roused his troops and headed south toward Columbia en route to his crossing site over the Cumberland River. At about the same time that Morgan left Campbellsville, Hoskins departed from New Market in pursuit of the raiders.

As Captain Simms' men in Morgan's column moved along in their saddles, additional Springfield men on opposite sides made their presence felt. The 1st Kentucky Cavalry Regiment with Springfield men in its ranks, coiled and ready to strike, waited in Greensburg. They were just a few miles off Morgan's right flank.

All day out in the column, raiders heard artillery roaring in the distance above the clopping of hoofs on the road. Duke wrote, "There was no cannonading going on—at least, in the volume which they declared that they heard—except at Murfreesboro, . . . but it seems incredible that even heavy guns have been heard at that distance." (Duke 1960, 342).

The big battle between Bragg's army of 33,000 men and Rosecrans' army of 44,000 men was raging at Stone's River near Murfreesboro, even though the railroad supply line for Rosecrans was out of action. Mattie was in Murfreesboro as the battle roared and thundered. In a letter she told Morgan, "I had some dark days dearest, and when the battle was raging around me in such furry, . . . there was one continual inquiry at the front door—'When will General Morgan be here?'" (Ramage 1986, 147).

Arriving at Columbia by mid-afternoon, Morgan gave his men a rest stop to eat and to feed their horses. Feeling the pressure from the nearness of Union General Wolford's cavalry regiments at Greensburg and Hoskins' pursuit, Morgan decided to make another night march. It would be dark and cold but nothing like the ride out of Springfield. Missing would be the sleet and bad roads that had created the worst night of the war for the raiders.

By daybreak on January 2,1863, Morgan reached his

crossing site near Burkesville unmolested, where he sent a courier with dispatches to Murfreesboro and a letter to Mattie. In spite of the pressing problems of accomplishing his mission, while avoiding entrapment and destruction deep in enemy territory, Mattie often occupied space and thinking time in Morgan's mind. The separation from his bride grieved him and he longed to be near her. In one of several letters written during the raid he wrote,

> *How very anxious I am My own pretty one to see you again. It seems as if I have been months away. But rest assured, darling, No time shall be lost reaching you. . . . The greatest pleasure of my expedition . . . is the knowledge that our great success will gratify and delight you. Our success has far exceeded my expectation & if our Generals will have done their part of the work, then our common foe will have been driven out of the state"* [Tennessee]. (Holland 1942, 186).

In another letter he wrote,

> *"How anxious I am looking forward to the moment when I shall again clasp you to a heart that beats for you alone. Do not forget me my own Darling & rest assured that my whole thoughts are of you. . . ."*

Feeling secure after crossing the Cumberland River on January 2, 1863, Morgan moved along, according to him, "in easy stages." Learning that Morgan had crossed the Cumberland River, the Union commanders called off the chase.

At Stone's River, the three-day battle ended in a standoff with both opposing armies suffering heavy casualties. Each army's casualties amounted to nearly a third of their men. But it was Bragg who left the battlefield. Unaware of Rosecrans' pressing need to be resupplied, Bragg withdrew his battered army and moved southeastward to form a new defensive position around Tullahoma, between Murfreesboro and Chattanooga.

After the battle, a long train of demoralized refugees pouring out of Murfreesboro tagged along behind Bragg's troops. Somewhere in the column of civilians who were carrying their treasured possessions on wagons or in carriages, Mattie took her place.

At Confederate Gen. William J. Hardee's new headquarters in Winchester, Tennessee, Mattie learned of Morgan's safe return. She wrote, "Come to me my own Darling quickly. I was wretched but now I am almost happy and will be quite, when my precious husband is again with me. . . ." (Ramage 1986, 147).

At his Headquarters in Smithville, Tennessee, on January 8, Morgan reported,

> *I reached this point on January 5, with my command. The results of the expedition may be summed up as follows: The destruction of the Louisville and Nashville Railroad from*

Munfordville to Shepherdsville, within 18 miles of Louisville, rendering it impassable for at least two months; the capture of 1,877 prisoners, including 62 commissioned officers; the destruction of over $2,000,000 of United States property, and a large loss to the enemy in killed and wounded.

On January 4, 1863, while Morgan and his command approached Smithsville, Tennessee, to end his Christmas Raid, a large crowd of Halisy's friends gathered around his opened grave at the Saint Rose Cemetery, near Springfield, Kentucky for the final graveside services as they laid him in his eternal resting place. "Mrs. Oscar Walker, . . . attended the funeral." (S. J. Boldrick letter, Aug. 29, 1939).

His thin rounded-top grave marker reads,

"D. J. HALISY
COL. 6 KY VOL, CAVALRY,
AGED 32 YEARS WAS KILLED NEAR LEBANON,
K.Y. JAN. 1, 1863 IN A SKIRMISH WITH
CONFEDERATE FORCES UNDER MORGAN."

Col. Dennis Halisy's tombstone (right foreground) in the St. Rose Cemetery, located near Springfield, Kentucky. The old, imposing edifice in the background is the St. Rose Priory Church. Pres. Jefferson Davis, future President of the Confederacy, studied there (Saint Thomas Aquinas College) in an attached building no longer standing. Courtesy of Jimmie Earles, *The Springfield Sun*.

Epilogue

NEIGHBOR AGAINST NEIGHBOR and sometimes brother against brother was the nature of the Civil War for Kentuckians. Six months after the Christmas Raid, Springfield Union cavalrymen chased their neighbors through their hometown again. But this time they rode on through Kentucky, across southern Indiana, and on into Ohio. Confederate Captain Simms was captured in Springfield, his hometown. His Company K and the rest of Morgan's command was captured either en route to, or in Ohio. About half of Captain Simms' company was from Springfield, Kentucky and most of the other half from Lebanon, Kentucky. Prior to Morgan's Ohio Raid, Captain Simms had been captured in Wolfe County, Kentucky on March 9, 1863 and exchanged in April of that year. After his capture in his home town on July 6, 1863, he was sent to Johnson Island Civil War Military Prison in Ohio. According to his POW records the twenty-seven-year old officer was six feet tall, had dark hair, dark complexion, and blue eyes. After the war he returned to Springfield. At Saint Rose, he married Nannie Craycraft in 1866. They had seven children—six girls, one boy. He died in 1902. Nannie was a widow for thirty-two years.

The Springfield Union men along with their peers in the 10th Infantry Regiment distinguished themselves at the Battles of Chickamauga, Missionary Ridge, and Jonesboro (near Atlanta). After Colonel Harlan resigned his commission and turned his command over to Col. William Hays, from Springfield, he went on to become a judge on the United States Supreme Court. The Boyle County native gained fame after the war as the lone dissenter on the Plessy *v.* Ferguson decision. That United States Supreme Court ruling institutionalized segregation. Harlan's famous phrase, "Our Constitution is colorblind, . . ." in his written dissent, in May, 1886, would provide inspiration and energy for the successful civil rights movement in the 1960s, a century after the Civil War.

During the Civil war, Maj. James McCreary, CSA, rose to the rank of Colonel. After the war, he served as a state legislature, 1869-75. In 1875, he was elected Governor of Kentucky. And, in 1911, he was elected Governor of Kentucky again. In 1892, he served as a Delegate to the International Monetary Convention, Brussels. After that he served three terms as a US Congressman. He has a county named after him: it was the last county formed in Kentucky, 1912.

After Morgan's capture near Lisbon, Ohio, on July 26, 1863, he was incarcerated in a penitentiary in Columbus, Ohio. In late November, 1863, he escaped and reconstituted his command. On his fourth and final deep raid into Kentucky in June 1864, discipline broke down in Mount Sterling. Some men and officers got out of control, stores were looted, shelves emptied, and a bank was robbed of $70,000. Morgan's failure to control his troops' behavior and to conduct an investigation concerning the events severely tarnished his record. In and around Cynthiana, he suffered heavy causalities. Upon his return to Virginia by way of Morehead and Prestonsburg, he was suspended from command and ordered to face a board of inquiry on September 10, 1864. But early in the morning on September 3, while under an attack on his headquarters at Greeneville, Tennessee, Morgan was killed.

In the summer of 1863, George Eastin was captured during Morgan's Ohio Raid at Pekin, Indiana. Steven Wright, from Elizabethtown Kentucky, is writing a book about the Union's 6th Kentucky Cavalry and has done extensive research on the subject. According to him, Eastin knew there was a reward being offered for him for killing Col. Dennis Halisy. So, when he realized capture was inevitable he hid Halisy's sword under a log. He had been wearing the sword since the day he took it off Halisy's body. Afraid to reveal his name, he went to prison at Camp Douglas under the name of Pvt. George Donald. Three months later he escaped and rejoined his command. After the war ended, he fled to Canada. In 1866, the Fayette County native located in Louisville, Kentucky where he became a distinguished lawyer. One of his admirers, Judge M. R. Hardin of the Kentucky Court of Appeals, wrote a long poem about Colonel Halisy's last battle with Eastin. Shortly after Judge Eastin's appointment to the Kentucky Supreme Court in 1885, he died while in Rome, Italy, where he had gone hoping to improve his health.

References

Source information and a partial list of books and documents mentioned or quoted by the author:

The S. J. Boldrick Letter, August 29, 1939, to O. W. Baylor, is located in the Filson Club Library in Louisville, Kentucky.

I gave the W. C. McChord memoirs to the KHS Library in Frankfort, Kentucky. They named it, "William C. McChord's History of His Life." It has a lot of information about the Civil War in and around Springfield, Kentucky to include the Battle of Perryville and details about plantation life, slave-master relations, and activities and much more.

I gave a copy of the "Autobiography of E. L. Davison: August 15, 1901," to the KHS Library. Edmund Davison's unpublished book contains the same kind of information in the McChord document, plus what was going on during that period at the state and national level.

Brewer, James D. *The Raider of 1862*: Santa Barbara, California: Praeger, 1997.

Duke, Basil W. *A History of Morgan's Cavalry*. Edited by Cecil Fletcher Holland. Bloomington, Indiana: Indiana University Press, 1960.

Kentucky Adjutant General's Office. *Report of the Adjutant General of the State of Kentucky, U. S. Volunteers. 1861-1865*: 2 vols. Frankfort, Ky.: Kentucky Yeoman Publishing Office, 1866-1867; Repr. Utica, Ky.; McDowell Publication, 1987 1988.

Kentucky Adjutant General's Office. *Report of the Adjutant General of the State of Kentucky: Confederate Kentucky Volunteers. War 1861-1865*: 2 vols. Frankfort, Ky.: Kentucky Legislature, 1918; Utica, Ky.; Cook & McDowell, 1980.

Ramage, James A. *Rebel Raider*. Lexington, Kentucky: University Press of Kentucky, 1986.

Speed, Thomas. *The Union Regiments of Kentucky*. Louisville, Kentucky: Courier Journal Jobs Printing Co., 1897.

Southern Bivouac: A Monthly Literary and Historical Magazine. 1882, Kentucky Branch of the Southern Historical Society.

Wyeth, John Allen, M.D., LL.D. *With Sabre and Scalpel, The Autobiography of a Soldier and Surgeon*. New York: Harper & Brothers Publishers, 1911.

LaVergne, TN USA
22 September 2010
197870LV00004B/2/P

9 780982 745311